Bound for Home

Between the world within
and that without –
a narrow bridge
and steep redoubt.

Dust

BOUND FOR HOME

The Fort Camden Commission

Poetry by Nell Regan

Artwork by Monica Boyle

ARLEN
HOUSE

Bound for Home

is published in 2011 by
ARLEN HOUSE
42 Grange Abbey Road
Baldoyle
Dublin 13
Ireland
Phone: 00 353 86 8207617
Email: arlenhouse@gmail.com

International distribution
SYRACUSE UNIVERSITY PRESS
621 Skytop Road, Suite 110
Syracuse, NY 13244–5290
Phone: 315–443–5534/Fax: 315–443–5545
Email: supress@syr.edu

ISBN 978–1–85132–029–5, softback
ISBN 978–1–85132–039–4, hardback

Printed in Ireland

A Cork County Council Fort Camden Commission 2011

Contents

FOREWORD

Cllr. Tim Lombard,
Mayor of the County of Cork

Fort Camden, which stands at the entrance to Cork Harbour, is a site which has great historical, social and cultural significance for the people of Crosshaven and indeed Cork County itself. The present fortifications, which date from the mid-nineteenth century, were home to a significant number of military personnel and their families and the development of the nearby village of Crosshaven owes much to its proximity to the fort.

With the redevelopment of Camden as a heritage site under the leadership of County Manager, Martin Riordan, Cork County Council in 2010 took the imaginative step of inviting artists to respond creatively to the site, its rich architecture and history. Four artist-led commissions have resulted, of which this wonderful volume of poetry by Nell Regan is a part. These poems are complimented by beautiful, often wistful, images created by Nell's artistic collaborator in this commission, Monica Boyle.

Poet and painter have chosen to pick up on what Nell calls the 'imaginative signals emitted by Fort Camden', sifting through the historical record, personal photographs and even found traces in the contemporary site to find inspiration in the human and personal details which they have so successfully transformed into poem and image. The collection, in many ways, serves to remind us that this was not just a building designed to protect, but was a place in which real people, each with their own personal history, lived and worked. This process in which the real and imagined are combined and laid down, layer on layer, by Nell and Monica adds enormously to our understanding of the fort and its significance.

As Mayor of the County of Cork, I welcome the publication of *Bound for Home* and extend my congratulations especially to Nell Regan, her publishers at Arlen House, artist Monica Boyle, the Rescue Camden Committee and the many other people who have assisted in bringing this work to completion.

Acknowledgements

The author and artist would like to pay tribute to and give special thanks to all those volunteering and working to rescue Fort Camden who gave so generously of their time, expertise and memories, in particular Jim O'Rourke and Stephen O'Mahony, and from the Rescue Camden committee, Paul Brierly, Eileen Murphy, Marion O'Riordan and Gary Heslin. Many thanks to Ian McDonagh and Cork County Council, to Kieran Enright for writing the historical essay on Fort Camden and to Alan Hayes of Arlen House for his dedication to continuing to produce beautiful books.

Nell Regan would like to acknowledge Eiblish Buckley and family for their hospitality and for always being able to answer or find an answer to questions, practical as well as historical. Special thanks to Monica Boyle, and to Tom McCarthy for an early reading of the poems. Two books in particular, both by local historian and folklorist Diarmuid Ó Murchadha were invaluable as a source of references and ideas: *The History of Crosshaven* (Cork Historical Guides Committee, 1967) and *Crosshaven: A Literary Portrait 1750–2000* (Crosshaven Development Committee, 2001). Thanks are due to Cathy Henderson, Maggie Regan, Ronan Foley, Paula Shields and Fíona Ní Chinnéide for critical advice and support throughout the writing and completion of this commission.

Monica Boyle would like to acknowledge the following people who have been invaluable in the realisation of this project, giving freely of their time, information, archives and support:
Shadow Box Frames, Chris Doswell, www.doswellgallery.com
Photography by Phil Pound, www.philpoundphotography.com
Imperial War Museum, www.iwm.org.uk
Ann Davoren, Director, WCAC, www.westcorkartscentre.com
Ian Humphreys, Artist
Caroline Knight
Vicki Aston
Paul, Amelia, Sophie and Sadbh Perry

INTRODUCTION

Nell Regan

My commission proposal was to write a series of short poetic monologues from the point of view of a range of characters connected in some way with the fort – human, non-human, historical and imagined. This would allow for the images and rhythms to present themselves over time spent at Fort Camden, in conversation, on research as well as through collaboration with visual artist Monica Boyle.

As I began to read and visit, the most insistent voices began to show up. First to arrive was the Monterey Cypress tree that grows in the fort – it reminded me of Rainer Maria Rilke's tree, 'always at the centre/ Of all that surrounds it'. Whatever military, political or social changes occurred in the fort over a near 160-year period, the Cypress continued and continues its yearly growth and it became a fixed point for the sequence. The whale arrived next and ends the poems back out at sea, to where the eye is always drawn at Camden.

Many conversations were had with the people who work, volunteer and live near the fort now, as well as those who grew up or trained there, about their relationship to the place and memories of it. Their (and my growing) affection for the place, the generosity and playfulness that this imposing military structure evokes, began to suffuse and lighten the sequence. Not only was there a local 'courting spot' just outside the fort, but it was also a rite of passage for teenagers from Crosshaven and farther afield to break into the tunnels, leaving behind a graffiti portrait of several generations.

It has been a very interesting process working in collaboration with visual artist Monica Boyle. Our preoccupations overlapped in many ways; we were both intrigued by daily lives lived in the fort and its surrounds, by the dereliction of the fort as well as its architecture, and both made extensive use of found archive material. 'Handover' was started after our conversations about the events surrounding 1938, and a productive afternoon spent at the fort looking at old military manuals provided material for two of the poems in the sequence.

Although sparked off by historical accounts and conversations, all the characters in the final sequence are fictional. Special thanks are due to Eileen Murphy for the repeated line in 'Hard Labour', "Those convicts were our slaves". Finally Kieran Enright's essay provides a valuable historical overview and context for the poems as well as the artwork.

– Fort Camden, July 2011

ARTIST'S NOTES

Monica Boyle

As I first visit Camden on a sultry summer afternoon with a group of other artists, I receive a warm West Cork welcome from our enthusiastic guides. I enter the grounds through heavily padlocked gates, surveillance cameras and 'keep out' signs warning of the consequences of illegal entry. Once inside, the imposing walls are a stern reminder of the redoubtable architects of this formidable building. The formal outstretched hand of the British Empire's colonial influence is almost palpable.

Despite the utilitarian function of the building, I am immediately struck by the sensitivity of design and attention to detail evident in the craftsmanship of cut stone and filigree ironmongery. Form and function have been given equal consideration. Constructed for endurance and longevity, this fine example of military fortification is here for posterity, and yet, as I walk through the grounds, it becomes clear that this monolithic structure is being slowly enveloped by nature; seed by seed, rhizome by rhizome, paths and parade grounds are being returned to a pastoral meadow of dandelions and daisies. It is a forbidden, enchanted garden in which nature is restoring culture to her nascent state.

I am captivated by the volunteers' colourful stories of U-boats and submarines, torpedoes and howitzers, rifle-ranges and railways, but am more than surprised to discover that no blood was ever shed at Camden. There is no taint of war here.

I step from bright sunshine into the cool, dusky interiors of the barrack building, my eyes gradually adjusting to reveal well-constructed rooms of elegant proportions, their walls a palimpsest of graffiti and peeling paints. The chilling emptiness serves only to remind me of activity and presence. A switch flicks in my mind's eye, running imaginary footage of soldiers sleeping, washing, dressing, cleaning. The soundtrack is the teasing banter of young men away from home for the first time. My eyes begin to focus again on the shards of glass which litter the floor inside and out, the smashed porcelain of sinks and showers, crumpled documents, rusting tools and the gaping holes of 'plunder'.

Over half of the fort's square surface area is beneath the earth. I descend into a labyrinth of underground tunnels and ammunitions stores which open into a large sepulchral magazine chamber, its austere design reminiscent of a Romanesque cathedral, with naves and cloisters of 'electricians' offices' and 'engine rooms' that serve as a monument to the men who tinkered there. I follow a rosary of torch lights as it winds its way tentatively through the maze of echoing darkness, and I emerge again into the light.

From the outset, my encounters with the fort have been laced with contradictions and paradoxes.

This first impression of light and dark, absence and presence, nature and culture, organisation and chaos, and the fragments and ruins of what had once been a highly ordered environment, have inevitably shaped my response to the fort. I have tried to create a piece of work which encompasses these contradictions. I have also attempted to give an insight into the ordinary activities of the men and women associated with Camden, and to conjure the rhythms, routines and relationships both within the fort and in its wider ties with Ireland and Britain

My work is concerned with themes of memory and legacy and employs the vestiges of our lives that we leave behind: mementos, letters, documents, photographs and artefacts. These everyday objects endure as remnants of our lives and provide a record of official and interpersonal interactions and relationships. In this body of work I have used archival records and materials which document the lives of the inhabitants of the fort in conjunction with the derelict objects found on the site. These artefacts are presented inside individual framed shadow boxes which are illuminated with low voltage lights to create a shrine-like presentation which alludes to the building's function as a monument to the past. The shadow boxes reference the tradition of presenting military personnel, upon their retirement, with boxes that contain medals, ribbons, photographs and flags to commemorate their lives and so I chose to use these to house the artworks, as I was to some extent commemorating the lives of the men and women who had lived there.

The boxes are exhibited in a large grid-pattern on the wall of the barrack room to recreate an archive. I am interested in how the archive functions as a repository of personal and cultural memory and I feel that an archival format gives a context to the fragmentary remnants of the miscellaneous material objects, without regard for their presence in time and history. Archives are themselves intrinsically paradoxical, oscillating between order and disorder, narrative and contingency, veracity and interpretation, what is present reinforcing what has been lost.

These glass-fronted boxes also allow for a random juxtaposition of found objects, text and imagery to create a visual poetry of infinite possibilities in which each viewer is invited to construct their own meaning. The boxes use objects and scripts, things that we can see, to provide a window into a world that we cannot see: a world of memories, ideas, fantasies and histories.

Collaborative Process

The realisation of these poems and artworks is the result of a high degree of collaboration between many people. In the beginning, we envisaged that it would be a simple process of me responding to the poems, and Nell responding to the shadow boxes, and this has certainly happened to a degree. *Truth, Dreams and History* and *All That Remains* are a direct response to the powerful imagery and pathos of *Handover* and *Hard Labour* respectively. Concerned that the works might become literal translations, we chose to work with broader themes and perspectives as there were obvious correlations in our interests. We have developed our work individually, but continued a dialogue about these subject areas. The sound installation of Nell's poems, which accompanies the exhibition, reflects a similarity of tone and atmosphere with the artworks.

Flowers are rarely pollinated by a single bee alone, and we spent several days with volunteers at Camden as they entertained us with stories about their relationship with the fort. Marion O'Riordan and her sister Eileen Murphy described how the fort was their home and playground, and Gary Heslin told us of his youthful adventures there with An Slua Muiri. All were generous with information, personal photographs and sourcing archival materials.

In the absence of any substantive archive, my pieces were increasingly dictated by the materials that I found at the fort. I am indebted to Jim O'Rourke and his gang for 'saving' the sacks of 'found objects', and for their hospitality, and to Paul Brierly for so kindly lending me his father's scrapbooks (works of art in themselves).

Thank you to Ian McDonagh for his support in bringing this project to fruition, to Nell for her glowing poems and to Arlen House for publishing the collection.

Thank you also to Ian Humphreys, Chris Doswell, Phil Pound, Ann Davoren, Caroline Knight and Vicki Aston for their generous support and finally to my husband Paul and my lovely girls Amelia, Sophie and Sadbh who make all of this possible.

Our imagination is stretched to the utmost, not, as in fiction, to imagine things which are not really there, but just to comprehend those things which are *there.*

– Richard Feynman,
Nobel Prize-winning physicist

Tree

The Monterey Cypress at the centre of Fort Camden was planted in 1854, at a religious ceremony, as a battalion of British soldiers left to fight in the Crimean War.

Ring No. 1
Who would have thought
that time could be marked so
in spreading and thickening bole?

Ring No. 10
I am a military tree, you see, a whiff
of grapeshot about me, *my spreading limbs*
commemorate Crimea, its each raw stump.

Ring No. 20
I could have been a god, I'll have you know,
a banyan or an oak in other days.
The private stubs out a butt on my trunk.

Ring No. 30
And then there was the endless sniping
of the natives – the ash, the oak, the yew.
What, the latter exclaimed, *you do death too?*

Ring No. 40
Unlike this fort, I am an engineering feat
fit for purpose. As it casts
the shadow of its own destruction, I flourish.

Ring No. 50
Through the hill I press deep
the fingers of my roots,
then farther into yielding soil.

Ring No. 62
News from afar floats on the breeze,
the seagulls talk of rebellion,
the jackdaws consider little else.

Ring No. 64
Consider the once mighty empire
of the Gymnosperm.
Fallen now. A clue, no?

Ring No. 66
Each midsummer smoke lifts
from the hills. As blood in water
blooms, descends, so it rises.

Ring No. 67
This year the city burnt for real.
The stench reached us here. Drunk
on carnage the Auxies exult.

Ring No. 70
Come the spring I might flutter
the eyelash of a cone at myself –
while a nostril of bark flares.

Ring No. 88
Abreast of us a liner glides.
The tricolour lifts. O Captain, herald this first time –
let each siren sound and the seas salute.

Ring No. 100
Call me *Palm*. Call me *Palm*.
Rest your eight year old hand
on my branch, now race the others to the gate.

Ring No. 110
Roy Orbison plays 'The Majorca' tonight!
as the *Dheis-Clé, Dheis-Clé* dies away
a murmuration of girls alight.

Ring No. 130
Shadows slip past: match flares, disappears.
Underground: butts, crumpled tins of beer.
On the wall: *'84. The punks of Togher were here.*

Ring No. 157
Do not be taken in by this sequence –
there exists a tree semantics, a syntax
you could not even conceive of.

SOUDAN
FRANÇAIS
Private and Confidential!
Monday
Another bright morning. It is a chance to
lie in bed until 8 in lovely weather
like this. Usual routine. Nothing much
doing. Only two eggs for breakfast.
Hopes of another joy-ride tonight.
Very dull and showery in the afternoon.
blankets out and fixing them up.
Ride cancelled. Don't know what to do.
Am thinking about the pictures but it is
too rainy.
Must go out. Have no one to write to.
News of rising in Cork.
One soldier drowned in the river here in
a boating accident. Cadet saved two.
My flowers seem to be coming up fine.
Off to pictures. Not much
chance of getting a girl.

Joy Ride

Tinker, Tailor…

The Timeless and the Rooted

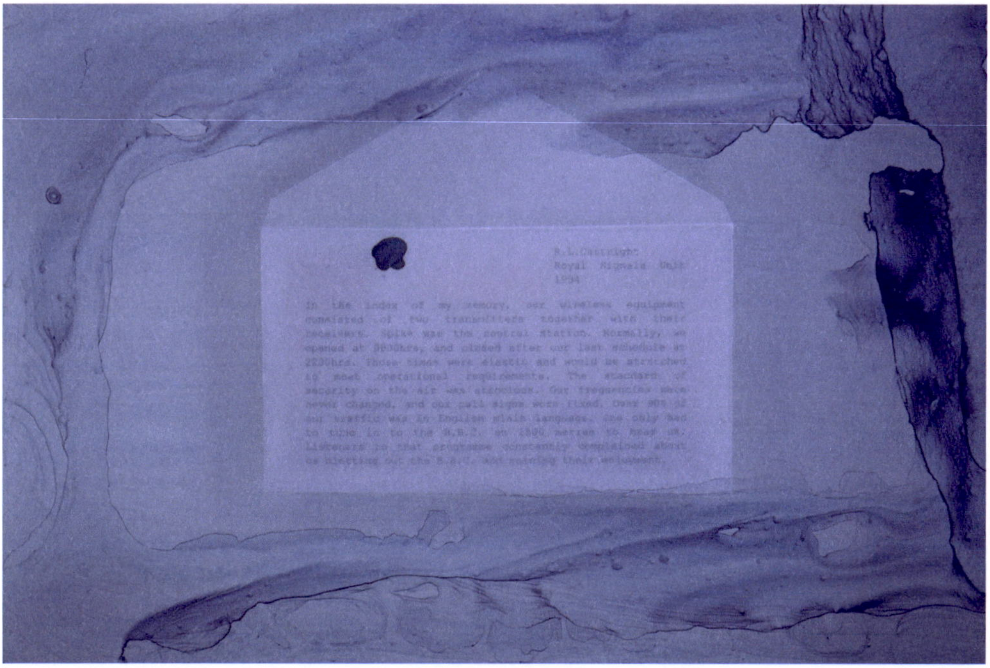

Interference

Disturbance

On the eastern point of land, close to the inner harbour, was a nearly perfect tumulus, which has been almost obliterated by the excavations for Camden Fort.
– Samuel Lewis, *Topographical Dictionary of Ireland,* 1837

They have slipped back in again.
Staked their claim again
in a sift, a shift, a settle of the soil
as a root hair sips beyond
prior reach. Through root
and living cell of sapwood
I know them – they have entered me.

Not the toiling line of convicts
I once espied in an angle of turning
through Camden volunteers,
nor even the officer who hung himself
in the rafters (there – the house
where balled lightning struck twice)
and their reappearance is certainly not

To be conflated with the tale
of the sí gaoithe, the fairy whirlwind
on Church Road, or the kind of a calf
with a jellied body whom it was death
to touch. No, these go further back.
Back to sea shells sucked clean –
a midden in our midst (or mist).

Here, they clamour up through my xylem,
here is the centre and the burial wound
or womb or mound, depending on the way
the wind moves and their inhumed sound
comes through me. All the while
the spiral stair of stone curves
and turns and orbits them unknown.

UNDER SIEGE

Fort Camden, though internationally recognised to be one of the world's finest remaining examples of a classical Coastal Artillery Fort, is sadly abandoned, derelict and overgrown.
– www.abandonedireland.com

The hill is swallowing the Fort.
Gorse scrambles up embankments.
Grass marches over battlements.
Willows mass in the moat.

The undergrowth rises up.
Dandelions billet in the officers' mess.
Heather chokes the cannon.
Spiders scuttle from the magazine.

Ivy blinds the pillbox.
Fern tips itself over ramparts.
Seagulls assess angles of elevation,
while on patrol slopes a lone fox.

With cracks that river out and down,
the map of the parade ground is being redrawn.

TOPOANALYSIS

In order to describe the psyche we have to describe and to explain a building, the upper storey of which was erected in the nineteenth century: the ground floor dates from the sixteenth century, and a careful examination of the masonry discloses the fact that it was reconstructed from a dwelling-tower of the eleventh century. In the cellar we discover Roman foundation walls, and under the cellar a filled-in cave, in the floor of which stone tools are found and remnants of glacial fauna in the layers below. That would be a sort of picture of our mental structure.
– Carl Jung

So, why don't you sit yourself down and tell me why you came. Yes. So all they ever say is you have *Seen no action* and *Never fired a shot*. I see. Interesting phraseology – what do you think lies beneath or behind that? Oh it's literal. You're a what? Yes, well I can see for a fort that would hurt a lot.

So, do you prefer Camden or Meaghar? I've never had a case like this before. Being honest is the way ahead I've found. I am prepared to take that first step with you and, yes, Jung's quote may well be our thread out of this mess, er, maze if I take on board your assertion that metaphor works both ways.

So well vaulted and constructed, hard to tell, you say, no room left, you say. Not sure if you are fort or hill? Well, integration is the key and for that we look to pre-memory. Little of you left I grant but wait, yes? The well? Tell me more. Naked rock that rears from vaulted tunnels, deep springs. Good. Good. We'll work with these things.

Abandonment? Twice? Then the broken teeth of your pier … voices in your tunnels at night … soles that won't fit the narrow steps of the past? Weekly sessions are the best shot here, er, idea – (this could take longer than I'd feared). We'll begin with your unrequited 'grá' for Roches Point. Next week? At four?

Recovery

Glue sniffing and alcohol abuse are now serious problems in Cork.
– *Irish Independent,* December 1986

I have tried to steer clear of the tunnels –
keep my mind where the mirror of the sea
beguiles the sky of the harbour –
but at night they burrow into my dreams.

The thickening wingbeat of the past
comes rushing toward me
as my feet begin their vertiginous descent,
grazing corners where dust remembers

and shadows spool off narrow steps.
The peeling paint of the magazine
is still afflicted by flashbacks.
I crouch where rust has daubed ochre

and dried blood. I bury my face
deep in the bag, inhale and wake in a sweat.

Now Sleep or Watch

All That Remains

Record and Prophecy

Angel's Verse

Hard Labour

There was a high mortality rate among convicts on the island, who were buried in unhallowed ground in unmarked graves on the west of island.
– *Séanad Debates,* Volume 184, 28 June 2006

Spike Island opened as a convict depot in 1847 and for many years after convict labour was used to expand and upgrade the fortifications in place at Camden and Carlisle Forts.

Those convicts were our slaves.
Forty years digging that moat –
for many it became their grave.

Spike, seen from night's quay,
incarcerates light at the harbour's black heart.
Those convicts were our slaves.

The fort, hewn of Crosshaven
Hill, leaves a gaping wound of redoubt.
For many it became their grave.

Seven years Justice gave
for a heinous crime of turnip-theft.
Those convicts were our slaves.

Iron huts, bibles, manacles to save
their 'sin-stained' hearts.
For many it became their grave.

Fenians, pick-pockets, the hungry, the depraved –
their histories suffuse the fort
which for many became a grave.
Those convicts were our slaves.

A Little Whimsy at the Heart of Empire

Or

Cork Harbour Shipping Intelligence

1847

Iona from Philadelphia
121 barrels Indian Corn Meal

Ajax steamer for Bristol
236 lambs
60 boxes of salmon
200 sacks of wheat
276 boxes eggs
5 casks of ham
25 bales of bacon
296 sheep
55 kegs butter

Ocean from Waterford
to embark with emigrants

1865

Arrived
Kaffirland, Calloa, guano
Onkel, Trinidad, sugar
Aurora, Bangor, manure
Celesta, Cardiff, coals, to Corfu

Sailed
Lizzie Anne from Alexandria
Seagull from Odessa
Helen, for London
Flying Cloud from Zalonica
The Exile from Alicante
Dante, for Galway

The Changing Moods of Fish

Or

Angling in Cork Harbour

Flounder and rockling,
conger, cod and tope.

Painted ray, golden-grey
mullet and gilthead bream.

Trigger fish and spurdog
thornback ray, bull huss.

Monkfish   ballan wrasse.

HANDOVER

Married quarters were built to accommodate the families of these soldiers, several of whom ... lie buried in the north eastern corner of Templebreedy graveyard.
– Diarmuid Ó Murchadha, History of Crosshaven, *1967*

On 11 July 1938, as British forces vacated the Treaty ports, the officers' dining room of Fort Camden was left laid, silverware polished and table linen pressed.

In the belly of the spoon
my thumb dips, makes
its circular motion;
my breath mists it, I burnish it
till, cradled in its curve,
my inverted face appears.

I catch the familiar dip
of her head as she pauses
at the window – I twist
to her un-misted reflection,
but in place of her dear back
are streams of laden soldiers

who pick their downhill way
to the jetty. Then, as if it
were the mirror we placed
to her mouth at the last,
I sup reflected light
from the spoon's mouth.

Truth, Dreams and History

Value of a Click

Re: Paints for Shells

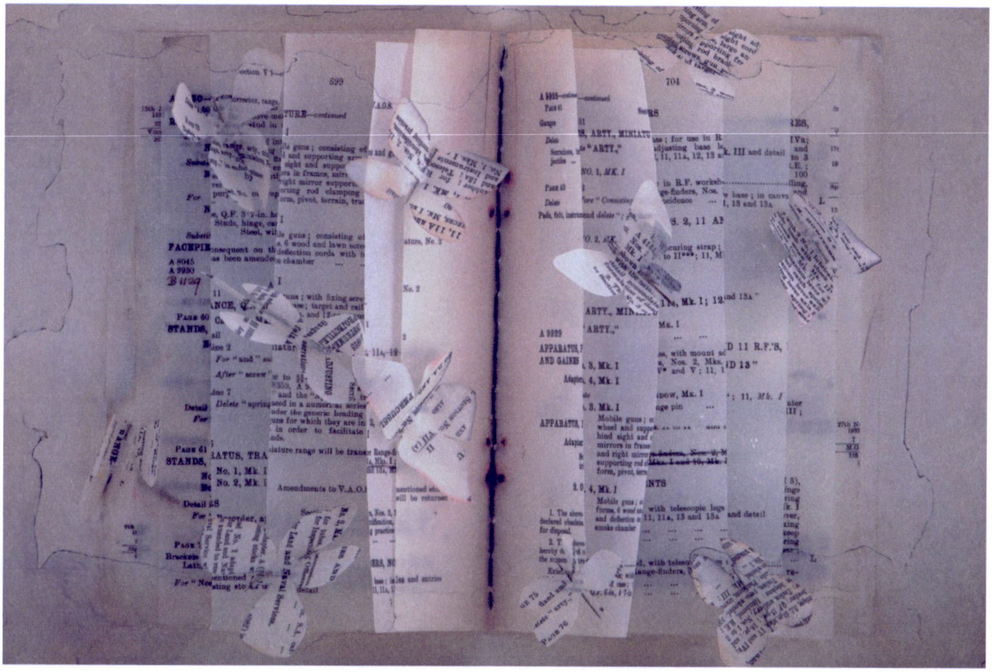

Changes in Nomenclature

SOFTENING THE BLOW

Or

MILITARY ACQUISITIONS MANUAL, 1934

4.5 inch howitzer
with felt jacket.

8 brass grommets
equally spaced
with a fastening lace
of Italian hemp.

In silk cloth
and shalloon bag
CARTRIDGES
BLANK.

A Night Out with the Navy

Or

Coast Artillery Training, Vol. 1, 1938

Rocking bar sights	opening of an action	comparative calibration
External ballistics	deflection for drift	jump and droop
Fall-of-shot	relationship of wear	curving depression.

Stencilled Above the Billet

War	Peace
60	30

The Ballad of Brennan's Torpedo

John Louis Brennan (1852–1932) was an Irish-Australian mechanical engineer and the inventor of the Brennan torpedo, the world's first practical guided missile. It was the most vital cog in Britain's coastal defence system and between 1884 and 1894, a series of 'Brennan's torpedo forts' were erected over harbours along the coast of Britain, as well as at strategic naval bases like Malta and Hong Kong. The only station to be built in Ireland was at Fort Camden, completed in 1895 at a cost of just over a million euro in today's money.
– www.palmerstonforts.org.uk

This scurrilous ballad bears no relationship to any of the events or people associated with John Louis Brennan. In fact the design of the torpedo was inspired by a cotton reel, tested in Sheerness, and as far as we know Brennan and his wife did not meet in Cork.
– Author's Note

As o'er the hills he came I could see,
such a fine man, what a gentleman he.
And he shew'd me his worth on one knee
John's eve, on the banks of the Lee.

My mother did chide me and spake
Take him childe, for the true man he be.
My consent so riled him he did take
me then and there. Layer upon layer

of clothing he perused till lace
shew'd. I kept my back to that wall
but my feet ne'er touched the ground
wrapped good around his stout base

Aim true, O Brennan, aim true.

We emerged from the escarpments,
my cheeks were rouged, my bonnet
did hang by one thread. By my smile
it was clear – Brennan was the man for me.

He did parade me on the grounds.
Billet me in the bushes.
Dispatch me in the dairy.
His kiss did honeycomb me

through and through and fill
each chamber with delight.
But, after we were wed
he did settle down to design by night.

Papers stretched wide on his desk –
to get good pleasure from him
I did taunt him as he sat intent.
Longer, Brennan, longer!

Harder, Brennan, harder!

He did spin on the wheels of that chair,
plump me on his lap, my sweet quim
dripped for him and my cunt yawned
wide to receive his goodly torpedo …

Oh yes, Brennan, oh yes.

After we spake of hydraulics,
of guided missile. *Look my love,*
I did say as I ran my hand along him,
such fine design here, my love ...

Out of his lying he lept
back to his sitting, back to his desk
leaving me lying alone –
our wedding bed grown cold.

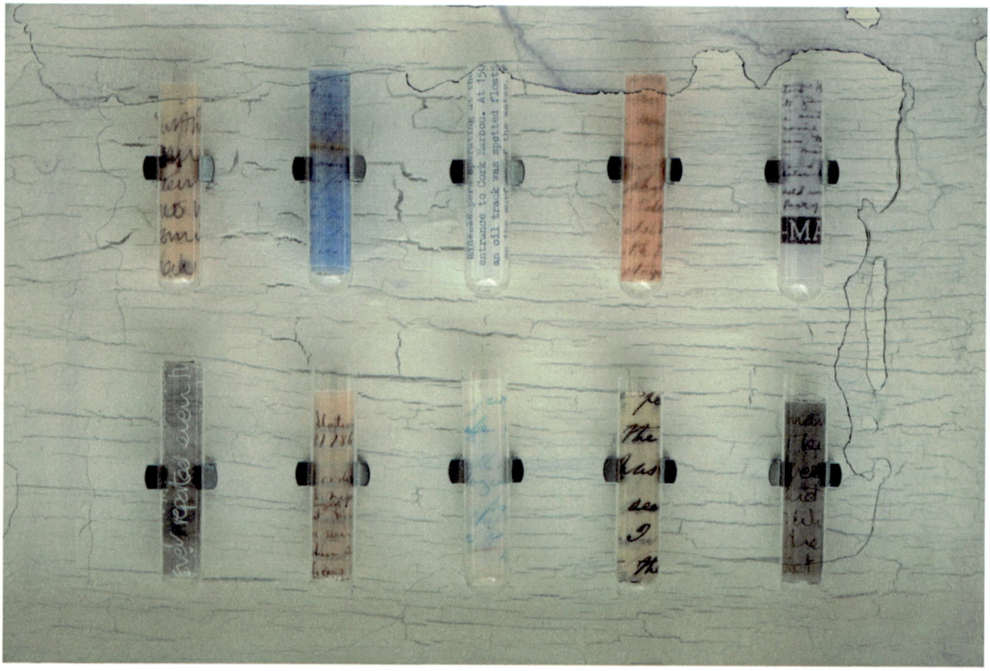

A Version of Events

Interference

The Story Told

Inclination

NEITHER CREATED NOR DESTROYED

Divers have described their discovery of a WWI German U-boat in 27m of water just off Roches Point. All 27 crew on board the UC42 died when the submarine sank at the entrance to Cork Harbour on 10 September 1917. It had been laying mines when an explosion was heard.
– RTÉ News, January 2011

Those dark days of the twentieth century
come rushing back through the estuary,
the tide filling its maw. Limbs
of the sea and fingers of the river
meet, thread through a rope
of all the tomorrows. The bay fills with light –
the long reach of the headland
ends in the thumb print of Roches Point,
or the X on a conscript's form.

Local sailors took me out, beyond land,
beyond Templebreedy. The bouquet
lifted and lilted on the waves when
a south easterly from Jutland harried us on,
asserted dominion. I groped
and juddered through the airless cabin.
Memory and synapses stall. I am but a body
pitching and lurching under it all.
It is my *grandmother's* face who appears.

On a Hamburg quay she stands. Leave over,
her lover left for waters unknown.
In her, tails lash through fluid
to destination, their time nearly up.
Egg ruptures through follicle
as eight hundred nautical miles away,
breath and outstretched hand release
and journey to the quay. The transfer
occurs like a fleck of foam thrown up.
It holds
          then drifts back down to sea.

Whale Song

On Sunday night at 8pm the batteries on Fort Camden and Carlisle opened fire on suspicious objects in the water believed to have been a German submarine. During the firing two of the shells from the batteries ricocheted off the water passing to the mainland of Crosshaven. One shell burst but the other did not. No harm was done by the shells landing on the mainland and nothing has transpired as to the effect of the engagement with the supposed unwelcome visitor to the harbour.
– *Southern Star*, January 1915

Squealing and keening it entered the sea,
seeking each breach of defence,
echoing beyond its reach –

how my soughing and spouting set it off
is not known. Ploughing through
the sound I thought I was bound for home

but when the sky darkened at four
I knew I had come too far
out of my glutinous, smooth waters.

It wheeled past me, air itself
splintered, the sea it cracked from side to side,
then bubbled and churned pig iron

so hearing smelted and fell in great
hissing drops to the sea floor. Song
stood still. Listening was lifted

on the swell and sucked back
into its vacuum. It set off a wave,
that gathered oceans to itself, collapsed as sound.

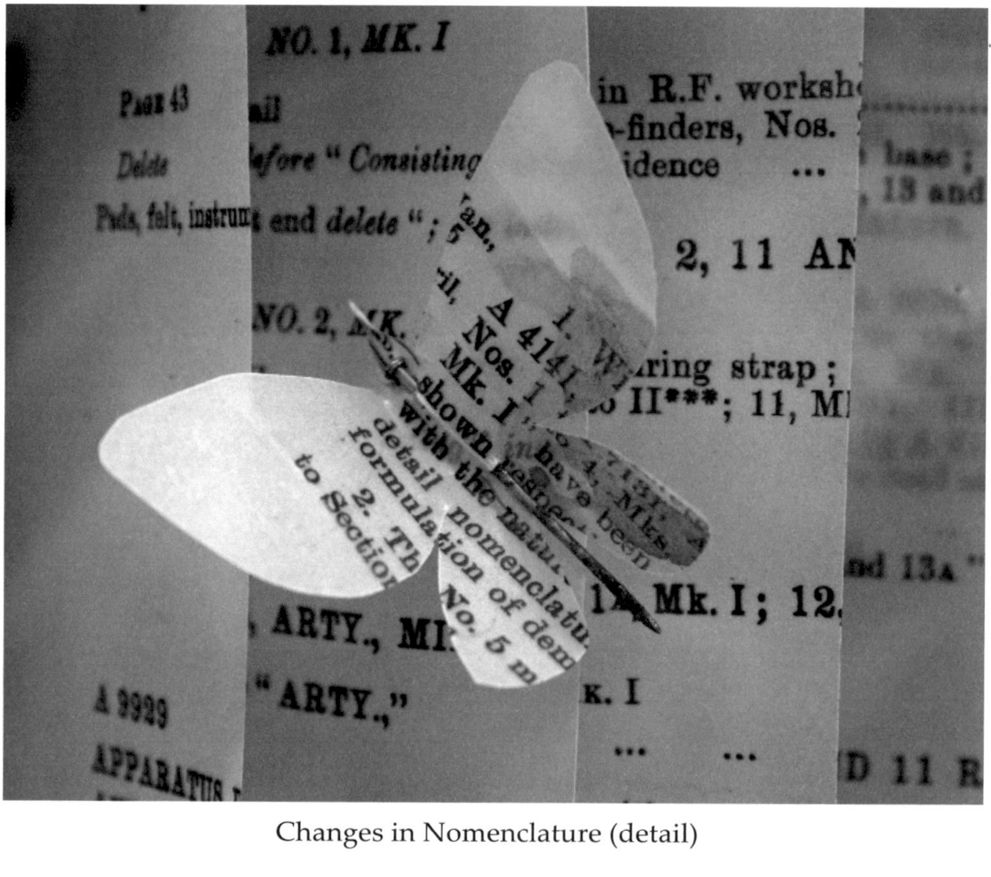

Changes in Nomenclature (detail)

Prisoners of Circumstance

Fort Camden: An Historical Perspective

Kieran Enright

Why do places, pieces of land, buildings interest us so much? How is it that as technology develops and communication intensifies we look back more than ever to our past? History is not just about great wars, battles, political conquests and upheavals. It is about people, people living their lives in places. The area around the site where Fort Camden sits never saw much of the great action that fills our historical consciousness, yet it has always stood there watching the world unfurl beneath it. Located on a hill at the narrow entrance to Cork Harbour, it was a site of major strategic importance for the British Empire and later the Irish Free State and yet, with the exception of several shots fired during the Williamite wars of the 1690s, the garrisons at Fort Camden never engaged in any military activity with enemy forces. It is, however, internationally recognised as one of the world's finest remaining examples of a classical coastal artillery fort and is currently undergoing regeneration.

Before 1860

The fort sits on Ram's Head, earlier called *Rinn Ramhar*, or the 'thick headland'. The first inhabitants of these shores may well have paddled into the welcoming waters of the harbour and we know that many middens, mounds of discarded shells, have been found in the surrounding area. A bronze-age burial site has been excavated across the water in Currabinny, and a tumulus or an ancient burial mound once existed where Fort Camden now sits. The area was well populated in the first millennium AD and, as well as several early church sites, there is ample evidence of *lios*es, or Celtic dwellings. The strategic and symbolic importance of the headland was marked early on, but it wasn't until the 1500s that the first fortifications were erected, to defend against an imminent Spanish invasion. During the Williamite wars in 1689–90, these fortifications were controlled by the Royalist forces of King James and shots were fired at William's ships as they entered Cork Harbour. The fortifications were extended in the 1780s with a full garrison and new batteries added in the 1790s as the threat of war with England's enemies intensified. In 1795 it was named Fort Camden after the Earl of Camden, Lord Lieutenant of Ireland. We can imagine the flurry of activity in the fort in 1798 as reports of French ships in Bantry Bay came through. However, with the defeat of the rebellion and, as the threat of war abated after Waterloo in 1815, a period of quiet resumed.

Fort Camden – Palmerston Fort

The present fort owes its construction to a major building programme of coastal forts around Britain and Ireland, instigated by British Prime Minister, Lord Palmerston. In response to the growing militarization in Europe and rapidly expanding French Navy, Cork Harbour was identified as a suitable navy port. It had easy access, safe anchorage and a strategic position, ideal for the defence of Ireland and the west coast of England and Wales. By the end of the 1860s, Fort Camden and its opposite number Fort Carlisle had been substantially rebuilt. Fort Westmoreland on Spike Island, in the centre of the Cork Harbour, was used as a convict depot from 1847 and much of the quarrying of stone and construction of the forts was done using convict labour. Fort Camden acted as an overflow prison and substantial numbers of convicts were housed in iron huts outside its walls.

Gaining access to Fort Camden by land requires crossing its deep moat by bridge and its isolation is clear. It occupies a sixty acre site, 200 feet above sea level, and walking past the casemented battery on the right and around the fort's other batteries, it is easy to imagine the daunting prospect it would have made for incoming enemies. When it was first built, over twenty guns of different sizes peered out of the batteries and more were added later. Because of the threat of artillery bombardment from enemy naval ships, access passageways were located underground. There are two separate tunnels from the upper batteries to the shore. From here, we can appreciate the fort's connectivity with Fort Carlisle across the water. Just over half a mile away, it was a simple and quick crossing.

Underground, an intricate spiral staircase leads down to the magazine while the temperature of the munitions room remains constant as no natural light is let in. A natural well is also located underground and this serviced a highly developed water system running throughout the fort. Other rooms built included messes, kitchens, workshops, stables and quarters for officers. For recreation, there was a tennis court, a skittle alley and a ball alley. These same features can be seen in Palmerston Forts all over Britain and Ireland, but Fort Camden is a particularly well preserved example. By the mid 1870s Europe's military and political alliances had shifted and the forts were already being deemed a waste of money and lampooned as 'Palmerston's Follies'.

Brennan Torpedo

Another notable feature of Fort Camden is that it hosts the remains of a Brennan Torpedo. This was one of the world's first guided missiles and was invented by John Louis Brennan, an Irish inventor living in Australia. In the 1880s it was installed across the British Empire. It could travel at over 30mph and hit an object over a mile away. Brennan and his team developed the torpedo in complete secrecy and, despite their best efforts, no foreign power managed to replicate it. The cost of installing the torpedo station at Camden was £9,225 (over one million euro in today's money). The torpedo's engine room still exists at Camden and the remains of the slipway used to launch it can be seen from the shore.

Fort Camden and Crosshaven Life

The fort's construction coincided with a boom in the fortunes of Crosshaven. Steamers from Cork, known as Green Boats, started ferrying day-trippers as new roads opened to Graball and Church Bays. A train service from Cork to Crosshaven opened in 1904. Hotels, refreshment rooms and an array of other businesses sprang up. A Sunday stroll along the seafront in Crosshaven in the early 1900s would surely have been something to behold – day-trippers from the city discussing the merit of John Redmond's Home Rule Party, a wife of one of the South Cork militia hopping off a Green Boat to meet her husband, an array of English regional accents as some Royal Engineers take the day off while the prospect of war in Europe looms. A glance at the census of 1901 shows a list of predominantly English names stationed at Fort Camden. Amongst them, a H.L. Chamberlain and a C.F. Hazeldin, 15 and 16 years of age respectively, their occupation listed as Buglers.

World War One

Fort Camden was heavily manned during World War One. As German U-boats disrupted Atlantic crossings, gunners remained on constant alert. On 7 May 1915 the real threat of German U-boats along Ireland's southern coast was realised when the *Lusitania,* a Cunard Liner was sunk twelve miles off the Old Head of Kinsale. 1,198 people died with her, including almost a hundred children. After a hostile American reaction, U-boat activity was scaled back for a period until after the Battle of Jutland and the launching of unrestricted submarine warfare. The naval war was now concentrated in the waters to the north and south of Ireland and when the US entered the war, the Navy established its European headquarters in Cork Harbour. In 1917 a U-boat was sunk off Roches Point by the explosion of its own mines. War ended but the strategic importance of Fort Camden and the other harbour forts continued to play a crucial role in Anglo-Irish relations until after World War Two.

Between World Wars

After World War One, Crosshaven and Fort Camden found themselves in an unusual position. When we think of the War of Independence in Cork, we think of Michael Collins, of Terence MacSweeney and Tomas Mac Curtain, of the burning of Cork and Barry's flying column. There is much evidence, however, to suggest that Cork was far from a rebel county in places. Complaining of the lack of support in 1920, Florrie O'Donaghue, the IRA's chief intelligence officer in Cork was able to say: 'The population of Crosshaven is, almost to a man hostile' (cited in Gerard Murphy, *The Year of Disappearances: Political Killings in Cork 1921–22*).

When the Anglo-Irish Treaty was signed in 1922 and the Irish Free State established, the Cork Harbour forts, Camden, Carlisle and Westmoreland remained in British hands along with the ports in Berehaven and Lough Swilly, known collectively as the Treaty Ports. So, between 1922 and 1938, while the Irish Free State flew the tricolour in other parts of Ireland, the Union Jack flew proudly over Fort Camden. This didn't seem to cause much concern. Indeed as the world economy crashed in 1929, local businesses were glad of the economic spin-off that came with the British fort. There was, and still is, a regard for the way the British did their business. The way in which the British left the fort in 1938 is always mentioned and we hear accounts of the silverware left shining on the tables, a world of perfection and order being gracefully left behind. However, Fort Camden in this inter-war period was not a compound totally divorced from regular life. The Crosshaven soccer team, made up mainly of Royal Engineers stationed at Camden, played in the Munster Senior League. In 1926, we see them losing two consecutive games to Cobh Ramblers and Cork City.

After the Handover

The Irish Free State took control of the Treaty Ports in 1938. Winston Churchill, who would take over as British Prime Minister a year later was furious at the handover. In a speech in the House of Commons, he referred to the Cork Forts as 'sentinel towers of the western approaches, by which the 45,000,000 people in this Island so enormously depend on foreign food for their daily bread'. Fort Camden was renamed Fort Meaghar, after the Young Irelander Thomas Francis Meaghar, but has remained Fort Camden in popular and official parlance. Throughout World War Two or the Emergency, Camden was under the control of the Coast Defence Artillery of the Irish Army and was also the centre of the Local Defence Association who were responsible for the immediate defence of the Crosshaven area. The CDA was disbanded in 1952 and after this the fort was used for summer training camps for An Slua Muire, the Naval Reserve. Images and stories from these times occupy the living memory. The fort was also the home to a series of caretakers and their families.

Dereliction and Regeneration

After the Irish Defence Forces vacated Fort Camden in the 1970s, it began to fall derelict. Plans at various times included the development of a luxury hotel, a heritage centre and an asbestos dump which was vigorously opposed by local people. Cork County Council took over the fort in 1989 but the site continued to lie unused. Over the past eighteen months, the newly formed and energetic Rescue Camden Committee, with the backing of Cork County Council and FÁS, have begun to transform Fort Camden from a decaying ruin into something bursting with potential.

Kieran Enright is a local historian and teacher of history and Irish at Colaiste Muire, Crosshaven, Co Cork.

Nell Regan

Nell Regan is a freelance writer based in Dublin. Her poetry is widely published in Ireland, Britain and the US and her debut poetry collection, *Preparing for Spring* (Arlen House, 2007) was shortlisted for several awards including the Glen Dimplex New Writing and Strong First Collection Awards. In 2010 she was the recipient of Literature Bursaries from the Arts Council and Dun Laoghaire/Rathdown County Council. In late 2011 she will be attending the International Writers Programme, University of Iowa as a Fulbright Scholar and International Fellow. She has also published historical biography and travel pieces.

Monica Boyle

Monica Boyle is a painter and exhibits throughout Ireland and England. She has exhibited at the National Theatre, London and has work in several national collections. Her work is concerned with themes of memory and legacy and focuses on the vestiges of lives and events that are now past or absent. Her most recent installation work uses personal mementos, letters, photographs and constructed archival materials to reflect on the traces of our lives that we leave behind.